The Comical Hash by Margaret Cavendish

Margaret Lucas Cavendish, Duchess of Newcastle-upon-Tyne was born in 1623 in Colchester, Essex into a family of comfortable means.

As the youngest of eight children she spent much time with her siblings. Margaret had no formal education but she did have access to scholarly libraries and tutors, although she later said the children paid little attention to the tutors, who were there 'rather for formality than benefit'.

From an early age Margaret was already assembling her thoughts for future works despite the then conditions of society that women did not partake in public authorship. For England it was also a time of Civil War. The Royalists were being pushed back and Parliamentary forces were in the ascendancy.

Despite these obvious dangers, when Queen Henrietta Maria was in Oxford, Margaret asked her mother for permission to become one of her Ladies-in-waiting. She was accepted and, in 1644, accompanied the Queen into exile in France. This took her away from her family for the first time.

Despite living at the Court of the young King Louis XIV, life for the young Margaret was not what she expected. She was far from her home and her confidence had been replaced by shyness and difficulties fitting in to the grandeur of her surroundings and the eminence of her company.

Margaret told her mother she wanted to leave the Court. Her mother was adamant that she should stay and not disgrace herself by leaving. She provided additional funds for her to make life easier. Margaret remained. It was now also that she met and married William Cavendish who, at the time, was the Marquis of Newcastle (and later Duke). He was also 30 years her senior and previously married with two children.

As Royalists, a return to life in England was not yet possible. They would remain in exile in Paris, Rotterdam and Antwerp until the restoration of the crown in 1660 although Margaret was able to return for attention to some estate matters.

Along with her husband's brother, Sir Charles Cavendish, she travelled to England after having been told that her husband's estate (taken from him due to his being a royalist) was to be sold and that she, as his wife, would receive some benefit of the sale. She received nothing. She left England to be with her husband again.

The couple were devoted to each other. Margaret wrote that he was the only man she was ever in love with, loving him not for title, wealth or power, but for merit, justice, gratitude, duty, and fidelity. She also relied upon him for support in her career. The marriage provided no children despite efforts made by her physician to overcome her inability to conceive.

Margaret's first book, 'Poems and Fancies', was published in 1653; it was a collection of poems, epistles and prose pieces which explores her philosophical, scientific and aesthetic ideas.

For a woman at this time writing and publishing were avenues they had great difficulty in pursuing. Added to this was Margaret's range of subjects. She wrote across a number of issues including gender, power, manners, scientific method, and philosophy.

She always claimed she had too much time on her hands and was therefore able to indulge her love of writing. As a playwright she produced many works although most are as closet dramas. (This is a play not intended to be performed onstage, but instead read by a solitary reader or perhaps out loud in a small group. For Margaret the rigours of exile, her gender and Cromwell's closing of the theatres mean this was her early vehicle of choice and, despite these handicaps, she became one of the most well-known playwrights in England)

Her utopian romance, 'The Blazing World', (1666) is one of the earliest examples of science fiction. Margaret also published extensively in natural philosophy and early modern science; at least a dozen books.

She was the first woman to attend a meeting at Royal Society of London in 1667 and she criticized and engaged with members and philosophers Thomas Hobbes, René Descartes, and Robert Boyle.

Margaret was always defended against any criticism by her husband and he also contributed to some of her works. She also gives him credit as her writing tutor.

Perhaps a little strangely she said her ambition despite her shyness, was to have everlasting fame. During her career, from the mid 1650's until her death, she was prolific. In recent decades her work has undergone a resurgence of interest propelled mainly by her ground-breaking attitude and accomplishments in those male straitened times.

Margaret Cavendish died on 15th December 1673 and was buried at Westminster Abbey.

Index of Contents

THE COMICAL HASH

THE CAST LIST
SIR WILLIAM ADMIRER
VARIOUS UNNAMED GENTLEMEN
LADY GADDER
LADY KINDELING
LADY BRIDLEHEAD
LADY EXAMINATION
LADY SOLITARY
LADY PEACEABLE
LADY FACTION
LADY CENSURER
MATRON

ACT I

SCENE I

[Enter a Company of **YOUNG GENTLEMEN**, and **TWO** or **THREE** young **LADYES**, as the **LADY GADDER**, the **LADY KINDELING**, and the **LADY BRIDLEHEAD**.

LADY KINDELING
My Dear Gadder.

LADY GADDER
My sweet Kindeling.

[They imbrace and kiss each other.

GENTLEMAN

Faith Ladyes Nature never made women to kiss each other, and therefore 'tis unnatural, and being unnatural it is unlawfull, and being unlawfull it ought to be forbiden.

LADY GADDER
Yes, you would have us kiss you men.

GENTLEMAN
No Ladies, we men will kiss you women, if you please to give us leave.

LADY BRIDLEHEAD
You will take leave sometimes.

GENTLEMAN
'Tis when we think we shall not be refus'd, or at least not to be disfavour'd for it.

[The **LADYES** kiss again.

GENTLEMAN
What, kissing again? faith Ladies you will make us believe by your often kissing, that you desire we should kiss you, and with that belief we may run into an error, if it be an error to kiss a fair Lady.

LADY KINDELING
Fye, fye, you men are odd Creatures.

GENTLEMAN
No, you women are odd Creatures, when you are not with us men.

LADY KINDELING
Preethy Gadder and Bridlehead let us go do something to pass away our time.

LADY GADDER
What shall we do?

LADY BRIDLEHEAD
Let us go to Cards.

LADY GADDER
Faith I have made a Vow not to play for money.

LADY BRIDLEHEAD
We will play for Sweet-meats.

LADY KINDELING
No, preethy let us play for a Sack Possit.

LADY GADDER
O no, we will play for Sweet-meats.

LADY KINDELING
I say a Sack Possit.

LADY GADDER
Let the most voices carry it.

GENTLEMAN
I will speak for the men, we say a Sack Possit, for that will make us both good Company in the eating the Possit, and after 'tis eaten, whereas Sweet-meats will make us heavy and dull.

LADY GADDER
Well then let us go play for a Sack Possit.

LADY BRIDLEHEAD
Faith a Sack Possit will make me drunk.

GENTLEMAN
You will be the better Company Lady.

LADY KINDLING
Fye Bridlehead, you should not say drunk, but your head giddy.

GENTLEMAN
That is better than to be drunk: for a giddy head hath a light heel.

[Exeunt.

SCENE II

Enter **TWO GENTLEMEN**

FIRST GENTLEMAN
The Lord Poverty is a gallant Noble person.

SECOND GENTLEMAN
They are gallant and Noble that are Rich, and titled Honour without Means, is like a Body without a Soul.

FIRST GENTLEMAN
You are mistaken friend, it is rather a Soul without a Body.

SECOND GENTLEMAN
Alas titled Honour without Means to maintain it, is despised.

FIRST GENTLEMAN
If the person hath Merit worthy of his titled Honour, that titled Honour is worthy to be respected and bowed to by all inferiour persons; nay put the case that Honourable titles are placed upon Unworthy

persons, yet all ought to give respect to those Titles, and to do homage thereunto, though not unto the Person, yet because it comes from a lawfull and Supreme power; as Natural rays of light do from the Sun; and those that strive through envy and through spite, for to Eclipse the light, deserve to be in a perpetual darkness; so those that do detract from titled Honours, ought never to be honoured with Titles or respect.

SECOND GENTLEMAN
Why, 'tis not only I that have no such titles of Honour that speaks against them, but those that do possess them, and their fore-fathers long before them.

FIRST GENTLEMAN
They that do so ought to be degraded, as being unworthy to wear the badge or mark of their fore-fathers Merits, or heroick Acts, for they do shew they have none of their own; but those that get their own Honours, by their own Merits and worthy Actions, deserve them best; for they, like as a clear and glorious day, appear; for oft-times their posterity, like Clouds begot from gross and drowsie Earth, strive to quench out their Fathers flaming Honours, and by their Baseness obscure the light of their fore-fathers great and glorious Fame, and in the end bury themselves in dark Oblivion, as vanishing to nothing, as being never mentioned nor remembred; but those that for their loyalty and their fidelity unto their King and Country, have hazarded lives, and lost their liberties and Estates, and are grown poor for Honesties sake, and Virtuous causes, yet they in after Ages will live with great renown; for 'tis not in the power of spite to pull them down; for the Gods give Fame to Noble Actions, as Kings give titled Honours; though men that are base will not relieve them, yet Fame will remember them; and though base men will rail against them, yet Fame will praise them; and though they dye with Poverty, and should end their lives in a foul Ditch, yet shall that Ditch be honoured by their Death, more than the rich unworthy man be honoured by his stately Tombs and costly Funerals.

[Exeunt.

SCENE III

Enter the **LADY SOLITARY**, and the **LADY EXAMINATION**

LADY EXAMINATION
What's the matter with you to day Lady Solitary? you look as if you were in a married humour.

LADY SOLITARY
Why Lady Examination, what humour is a married humour?

LADY EXAMINATION
Why a masse of ill humours mixt or put together; as a lumpish, dumpish, dull, stupid humour; or a pievish, fretting, pining, whining humour; or a brawling, yawling, cuarrelling, scoulding humour; or a jealous, suspicious humour; or a fawning, feigning, dissembling humour.

LADY SOLITARY

If these humours are woven into the marriage knot, I will never marry, for I would be loth to have the peace of my life strangled in discontent: for whosoever be subject to these humours can never be happy.

LADY EXAMINATION
You will change your mind, and rather live with these humours than without a Husband; but I am come now to fetch you abroad, for their is a Company of sociable Ladyes and gallants, that have made a meeting some league of, where there will be Mirth, Jollity, Plenty and Pleasure, and they desire you will be sociable for once, and go along with them.

LADY SOLITARY
Would you have the Body which is the habitation of the Mind a wanderer, travelling from place to place, disturbing the mind with unprofitable journeys?

LADY EXAMINATION
No, I would have it remove so as it may always situate itself in a wholsome, profitable, plentifull, pleasant, and pleasurable place.

LADY SOLITARY
I perceive you prefer the pleasures of the Body before the delight of the Mind.

LADY EXAMINATION
Why the mind can take no delight without the body; for the body gives the mind a being and habitation: for there would be no mind if there were no body, but if there could be a mind without a body, yet the mind could receive no delight without the pleasure of the body, for the pleasure of the body is the delight of the mind, and not the delight of the mind the pleasure of the body, for the mind doth never give nor return; wherefore come away, and leave your Solitary musing to those whose condition of fortune denies them the use of the World, and worldly pleasures, and do not deny your self, for I hate a self-denying Creature.

LADY SOLITARY
Well, you shall prevail with me for this one time.

[Exeunt.

SCENE IV

Enter **TWO GENTLEMEN**

FIRST GENTLEMAN
Have you seen Monsieur Thesis Book of Poems that is newly come forth?

SECOND GENTLEMAN
Yes.

FIRST GENTLEMAN

And how do you approve of them?

SECOND GENTLEMAN
As well as I do of an Anagram.

FIRST GENTLEMAN
There is never an Anagram in the Book.

SECOND GENTLEMAN
Why the whole Book is an Anagram of Doctor Costives Poems: for he hath only new placed the words, as they do Anagrams of names, but the whole matter, sense, and conceits is the same.

FIRST GENTLEMAN
Indeed he hath imitated him.

SECOND GENTLEMAN
By your favour, imitation is only to be like another, and not the same: but his is the very same, as I have told you, for which he deserves less praises than a Imitator, although those that do imitate any Excellent Poet, do nor gain so much honour to themselves, as they give honour to those they imitate; as for example, the Imitators of Homer give more honour to Homer than to themselves; for Imitators are only as Painters, where he that is imitated is as Nature, or the Gods, for the one draws but Copies, the other makes the Original; so that there is as much difference as a Man, and the Picture of a man.

FIRST GENTLEMAN
But a Painter that draws the Picture of a man, very like the life, he may be more famous than the man that is drawn.

SECOND GENTLEMAN
But not worshiped and adored, as Nature is, that made him: for Art cannot out-do Nature, nor do as Nature hath done, and doth do; and an Imitator is but an Artificer, when as the Original Author is a Creator, and ought to be accounted of, and respected, and worship'd as Divine; but there are or have been but very few Poets that have such powers and parts to make a perfect Creature, which is a perfect work, as Poems, scenes, or story; but some Poets are like Chymist, that strive and labour to make as Nature makes, but most fail in their work, and lose their labours, wanting that Natural heat, or well-tempered matter, which should produce such Creatures as Nature makes, yet some 'tis said have made gold, as Raimond Lully.

FIRST GENTLEMAN
Then Homer is a Raimond Lully in Poetry.

SECOND GENTLEMAN
Nay rather Raimond Lully is a Homer in Chymistry: for no man ought to compare Homer to any Creature, by reason he hath out-wrought Nature, having done that which she never did; for Nature never made Gods, Devils, Hells, and Heavens, as Homer hath done.

FIRST GENTLEMAN
For my part I had rather be Raimond Lully than Homer: for I had rather have the Art to make Gold, than the Nature to make Poems.

SECOND GENTLEMAN
You would not gain so much by Gold as Wit.

FIRST GENTLEMAN
Why, what shall I gain?

SECOND GENTLEMAN
Fame.

FIRST GENTLEMAN
But Gold will bribe Fame to speak as I would have her, if I have gold enough to bribe her.

SECOND GENTLEMAN
But Poems will force Fame to speak for you without a bribe.

FIRST GENTLEMAN
That were all one to me, so she speaks well, whether she be forced, flattered, or bribed.

SECOND GENTLEMAN
But there is a fate of Poverty on Chymists, as much as on Poets, so that if you were as Excellent a Chymist as Raimond Lully, you would be as poor as Divine Homer.

FIRST GENTLEMAN
Not if I could make Gold.

SECOND GENTLEMAN
Yes, for Chymists spend more in the making of Gold, than they gain by it when it is made; and how should they do otherways, when they must needs spend a pound or pounds to make a grain? for the limbeck of a Chymist is but a little Still set a-work by a wasting fire, whereas Natures limbeck is the Earth, set a-work by an undecaiable fire, which is the Sun; this Chymist becomes as poor by an over-greedy Covetousness, as Poets by a despising Carelessness.

FIRST GENTLEMAN
Then Chymists are like those Bodyes which become lean with over-eating, and Poets like those Bodyes that becomes lean by over-fasting; the one surfits, the other famishes.

SECOND GENTLEMAN
Indeed Chymists are so greedily Covetous, and feed so much on hopes, as they never leave untill such time as they have vomitted out all their wealth, and then they become sick and lean with Poverty.

[Exeunt.

ACT II

SCENE V

Enter **TWO** other **GENTLEMEN**.

FIRST GENTLEMAN
The Lady Faction is of a strange busy Nature, she runs into every House, takes upon her to govern every ones Family, yet cannot rule her own; she condemns all Actions, be they never so Just or Prudent; all Officers, be they never so worthy, or fitly placed; all Laws, be they never so beneficial, or expedient for the Common-wealth; all Customs, be they never so antient or harmless, indeed all peaceable, wise, and well ordered Governments: she hates and delights in nothing but disordered change.

SECOND GENTLEMAN
'Tis said she is in love with Sir William Admirer.

FIRST GENTLEMAN
And he in love with the Lady Peaceable.

SECOND GENTLEMAN
She is a sweet Lady.

[Exeunt.

SCENE VI

Enter the **LADY PEACEABLE**, and **SIR WILLIAM ADMIRER**.

SIR WILLIAM ADMIRER
I will sit and lissen to what you say, and learn from you what is the noblest way to entertain the life.

LADY PEACEABLE
Alas I cannot learn you, I have not long experience, my Soul is young, a meer novice Soul, it wants both growth and experienced years, for I am like a House that is newly built and is unfurnished.

SIR WILLIAM ADMIRER
Though you are young, you are wise.

LADY PEACEABLE
How can you expect youth can be discreet and wise, when those that have lived long, and have had much experience, are oftentimes Fools? wherefore I can only entertain you like a Parrot, only with words, not wisely to discourse, and if you should lissen to me long, I shall surfit your Ears with idle words, for the Brain will be as soon over-charged with noise, as the Stomack with meat.

SIR WILLIAM ADMIRER
I can no more be weary of thy words, than Angels are with Heavenly Musick.

[Enter the **LADY FACTION**.

LADY FACTION
Lady Peaceable, the report is you are Ambitious to get away my Servant Sir William Admirer from me.

LADY PEACEABLE
I am only Ambitious to live Virtuously, and dye Piously.

LADY FACTION
Why Servant, I hear you have forsaken me.

SIR WILLIAM ADMIRER
I despaired of ever being entertained, and so I never really address'd a Sute, but by way of rallery.

LADY FACTION
Your Mistriss doth not believe you, for she blushes either for your faults, or her own.

LADY PEACEABLE
My Bashfullness proceeds not from a Guiltiness, either of base actions, wicked thoughts, mean birth, or breeding, or evill or erronious opinions; for my bashfullness is only an effect of Nature: for as some are naturally fearfull, so am I naturally bashfull; and as Melancholy produces a sad Countenance, so Bashfullness produceth an extorted and a Convulsive Countenance; as Grief produces tears, so Bashfullness produces blushing.

SIR WILLIAM ADMIRER
Lady Faction, spare my young Mistriss, lest she should out-run you in a full speed.

LADY FACTION
Your Mistriss is too grave, and speaks too scholastical for a woman, she seems as if she had been bred in an University, which breeding is fitter for a man.

LADY PEACEABLE
No surely, for men should be bred with Heroick Actions, women with Modest Contemplations, as I have been.

LADY FACTION
If you have talk'd so seldome, and have learn'd so little, how come you to know so much?

LADY PEACEABLE
My knowledge is not copious, yet I have learn'd as much as my years could imbrace, and my desire is to know as much as Modesty will allow of, Honour will give leave to, Capacity can comprehend, or Life can reach at; but the longest life is but a short time to gather knowledge in; but Madam, I should think I had learn'd well, if I knew how to do you service.

LADY FACTION
Let me tell you, 'tis Craft and Subtilty that you practice, to catch fond, facil Fools under the veil of Civility, but not good Nature; for you, like a Sorceress as you are, Inchant and Bewitch all that come neer you, with this dissembling, for which you ought to be banish'd from all noble Company.

LADY PEACEABLE

Take heed Lady of sharp-headed Curses, that Shoot through Innocent Lips, they seldome miss the mark they aim at.

LADY FACTION
Shoot as many as you will, I fear them not.

[**LADY FACTION** goes out.

SIR WILLIAM ADMIRER
My dear sweet, wise, Virtuous Mistriss, be not angry, for all the World knows the Lady Faction is a disturber of all good and peaceable Society.

LADY PEACEABLE
No, I am not angry with her, but I will watch her, lest she should do me some harm.

[Exeunt.

SCENE VII

Enter the **LADY SOLITARY** as sitting a writing, then enter the **LADY EXAMINATION** as to visit her.

LADY EXAMINATION
Prethee what art thou writing?

LADY SOLITARY
I am writing Fancies.

LADY EXAMINATION
Prethee what are Fancies?

LADY SOLITARY
Why, Fancies are minzed Objects, pounded and chopt by Imagination, which Imaginations are the several Cooks which serve the Mind; and as skillfull Cooks of several meats make Bisks or Olioes, so doth the Imagination of several Objects; and as skillfull Cooks will mix several meats, so as not any one particular shall be tasted, so doth the Imagination of several Objects or Subjects.

LADY EXAMINATION
But some say Fancies are Created by Motion in the Brain, which would be there were there no such materials as Objects or Subjects, which the Senses as Caterers bring in.

LADY SOLITARY
The Brain can no more Create Fancy without the materials of outward Objects, and Subjects, than Nature can Create a World without matter to make it withall; so the Brain can no more Create Fancy without the help of the Senses, than Nature can Create a Creator without the help of Motion; for though Fancies are the works of the Brain, yet the Brain could not work unless it had something to work on; but Objects and Subjects of Objects, may be divided in the Brain so small, or beaten so thin, as the first form

may be beaten out, and when the first form is gone, we deny the matter, like as if we should deny that Paper is made with Rags, because the form of Rags is beaten out; thus by the subtill and curious motion of proud Conception joyned with the dazled memory, we deny the Senses a share, as not being Partners therein, or laboures thereof, the same way we conceive the Gods, for the Conceptions of the Gods is but minzed Imaginations.

[Exeunt.

SCENE VIII

Enter the **LADY CENSURER**, and the **LADY EXAMINATION**.

LADY EXAMINATION
Lady Censurer, pray what think you of the Lady Retorts wit, hath not she a great wit?

LADY CENSURER
Oh fye, she hath a Chamber-Maids wit.

LADY EXAMINATION
What wit is that Lady?

LADY CENSURER
Why a snip snaply wit.

LADY EXAMINATION
Indeed I have heard many Nursery Maids give so sharp and quick replies, as amongst some would be judged to be great wits, yet come to discourse seriously with them, and they were not much wiser than Beasts; but what do you think of the Lady Sharps wit?

LADY CENSURER
Her wit fetches the skin off of the Ears, it corrodes the minds of the hearers, more than Vinegar the tongues of the tasters.

LADY EXAMINATION
How approve you of the Lady Courtlyes wit?

LADY CENSURER
Her wit is tedious, as all Complementing wits are, they tire the Ears of the hearers.

LADY EXAMINATION
What say you to the Lady Stronglines wit?

LADY CENSURER
Her wit is costive, and is delivered with labour, difficulty, and pain.

LADY EXAMINATION

What think you of the Lady Learnings wit?

LADY CENSURER
Her wit is an Alms Tub, it yields nothing but scraps, fragments, and broken pieces.

LADY EXAMINATION
What think you of the Lady Subtilties wit?

LADY CENSURER
Her wit is Lime, Twigs, Snares and Traps to catch Fools in or with.

LADY EXAMINATION
How like you the Lady Fancies wit?

LADY CENSURER
Her wit indeed is a true Natural wit, it 'tis sweet and delightfull, easy and pleasing, as being free and unconstrain'd.

LADY EXAMINATION
How like you the Lady Contemplations wit?

LADY CENSURER
Her wit is wise, and distinguishing well: for all Comtemplative persons judge, weigh, and measure out the right and truth of every thing, and find out the easiest and profitablest wayes, by the help of consideration; yet Contemplative persons when they come into Company, or publick Societies, their tongues do as Boys, that having been kept hard to their studies, when once they get a play day, they run wildly about, and many times do extravagant actions: so Contemplative persons when they are in Company their tongues speak extravagant words, and their behaviour for the most part is unnatural to their dispositions; but of all wits the Contemplative wit is the best, by reason it is a neet Neighbour to Poetry.

[Exeunt.

ACT III

SCENE IX

Enter the **LADY GADDER**, the **LADY KINDELING**, and the **LADY BRIDLEHEAD**.

LADY GADDER
Come friend Kindeling, and friend Bridlehead, let us go to the Lady Censurers; for there is the resort of all the gallants at her House.

LADY BRIDLEHEAD
What should we do there? for all the men will hearken so much to her discourse, as they will take no notice of us.

LADY KINDELING
Why then we will take notice of them: for if we should stay at home, and not seek out the Company of men, faith we shall never get us Husbands.

LADY BRIDLEHEAD
It is easy to get the Company of men, not so easy to get Husbands: for we have a great many men that come often to visit us, but none offer to marry us.

LADY GADDER
But the more acquaintance we have, the more likely we should get Husbands; for it were a hard Fortune, if amongst so many men we should not got one Husband.

LADY KINDELING
Why one Husband will not serve us three.

LADY GADDER
I mean each of us one.

LADY BRIDLEHEAD
Well then let us go.

[Exeunt.

SCENE X

Enter the **LADY SOLITARY**, and the **LADY EXAMINATION**.

LADY EXAMINATION
Oh thou Clod of Earth, sit not idle here, but go abroad and receive the comfort of the Sun, which works to all effects.

LADY SOLITARY
I need not, for my Mind is as the Sun it self, and hath the same effects; for my Mind doth contract, attract, dilates, and expulses, for sometimes it dilates it self as the Sun doth, in beams of light, which is Inventions, at other times the Mind dilates, as the Sun his hear, which is in Poetick flames, and in rarified fancies; likewise the Mind attracts; as the Sun doth Vapours from the Earth, so my Mind attracts knowledge from the World, as from several subjects and objects, as the Sun from several Climates; likewise as the Sun contracts porous matter into a solid sustance, so doth my Mind contract loose thoughts into solid Judgment; and as the Sun expulses united Bodyes into parts, so doth my Mind expulse its serious Contemplations, and united Conceptions into several discourses.

LADY EXAMINATION
Prethee expulse this discourse amongst thy sociable friends.

LADY SOLITARY

What amongst the sociable Virgins?

LADY EXAMINATION
Nay faith, Wives for the most part are more sociable than Maids.

[Exeunt.

SCENE XI

Enter the **LADY CENSURER**, and a **GENTLEMAN**.

LADY CENSURER
Sir, I hear you intend to be a Souldier in the Wars.

GENTLEMAN
Yes Madam, I am come to take my leave, and to kiss your Ladiships hands before I go.

LADY CENSURER
Sir you have chosen an honourable Profession, for though it is an industrious, carefull, painfull, and dangerous Profession, yet it is a noble Protection to the Weak and Infirm, to the decrepid Age, and shiftless Youth; to the faint and tender Female Sex; it is a guard to the ashes of the Dead, and to the Temples of the Gods; for without Marshal Discipline no Peace would be kept, Truth and Right would be torn from the owners, Justice pull'd out from her Seat, and Monarchy quite from his Throne, and though a Souldier may lose his life sooner than Nature did determine, yet in recompence, Honour buryes him, and Fame builds up his Monument.

GENTLEMAN
Your descriptions Madam are able to make a Coward a Valiant Man.

[Exeunt.

SCENE XII

Enter **TWO GENTLEMEN**.

FIRST GENTLEMAN
Some have thought the World was but as Stage, and that the several Creatures are the several Actors, and that every several Generation is a new Play.

SECOND GENTLEMAN
No every several Generation doth not seem as if they were new Plays; for there seems to be but one play, and that to continue to the end of the World, and that every Generation seems only new Actors, that play over the same parts, for we well perceive that the following Generations act but what the former Generations did before them; 'tis true the World seems to be the Stage, and the Seas, Rocks,

Rivers, Plants, Hills, Dales, Cities, Towns, Villages, and the like, are as the several Changes, the Animals as the several Actors, the several Seasons the several Scenes, and the Spectators are the Gods, and the end of the World the end of the Play, and then they must make another World, if they will have another Play.

FIRST GENTLEMAN
Surely Mercury is their Poet.

SECOND GENTLEMAN
'Tis very likely, also 'tis probable Pallas helps him.

FIRST GENTLEMAN
Nay 'tis probable the Venus and Cupid helps him, for Love and beauty doth at all times assist a Poet.

SECOND GENTLEMAN
There is no excellent and extraordinary wit, but hath many assistants, as first Nature is the chief, so likewise Mercury, Pallas, Venus, Cupid, and the Muses.

FIRST GENTLEMAN
The most foolish Actors of all Actors, are women.

SECOND GENTLEMAN
The truth is, it 'tis very unhappy for women, that they are not instructed in the rules Rethorick, by reason they talk so much, that they might talk sensibly, whereas now for want of that Art, they talk meer nonsense.

FIRST GENTLEMAN
But all women are apt to speak more than to Act, by reason words are easily spoke, and deeds so hard to be done.

SECOND GENTLEMAN
Faith women are as full of Actions as words; for all their life is imployed with talking and running about to no purpose.

[Exeunt.

ACT IV

SCENE XIII

Enter the **LADY SOLITARY**, the **LADY EXAMINATION**, the **LADY CENSURER**, and a Grave **MATRON**.

LADY EXAMINATION
Come let us go abroad, for I love to refresh my self in the Serene Ayr, taking the pleasure of every Season, as when the returning Sun spins Golden Beams, which interwaves into the thiner Ayr, as Golden Threads with softer Silk, making it like a Mantle, Rich and warm, which wraps the Body of each Creature

in; so in the Summer when lifferous winds do fan the sultry heat; then in the Autum that's like a temperate Bath, which is neither too hot nor too cold; then in the VVinter, when freesing cold doth purge the Ayr, as Physick doth the Body from most corrupt humours, and binds each loose deshevered part.

LADY CENSURER

The Winter will bind up your active limbs, and numb your flesh, and make your Spirits chill, besides Winter doth bedrid Nature, 'tis a spightfull malicious and wicked Season, for it doth strive for to destroy each several thing, and it yields nothing good it self; besides it doth Imprison many things, binding them fast with Icy Chains, taking away their Natural Liberty, also it doth not only frown, and lour on the bright Sun, making his light dim and dusky, but Winter doth untwist, and doth unweave the Suns bright Golden Beams, and wind them on dark bottoms.

LADY SOLITARY

The cold sharp Ayr is as sharp unto the touch, as a Lemon to the tast, and works a-like in some effects.

MATRON

Yes be'r Lady in causing frowning, and crumpling faces.

LADY SOLITARY

Not only so, but sharp Ayr, and sharp Lemons, do both cleanse from Putrification, and keep from Corruption.

LADY CENSURER

But hot Ayr works upon the Body, as stronge Liquors upon the Brain, for hot Ayr distempers the Body, as strong Liquors do the Mind.

MATRON

Beshrow me, I have felt some Ayres as hot, and as burning, as Brandy-wine.

LADY SOLITARY

What Wine is that?

MATRON

The Wine of Wine, the Spirits of Wine.

LADY CENSURER

Indeed that Wine, if you call it so, which is Strong-waters, will work upon the Body as soon as the hottest Ayr, causing Feavours and other Malignant diseases.

LADY EXAMINATION

It seems that hot and burning Ayr, works upon the Spirits as much and as soon as the hottest Liquors, and hot Liquors upon the Body as much as hot Ayr, both causing Feavours and Frenzies.

MATRON

In truth, and I heard that Ayr is liquid, and so is Drink, and Drunkards, like frantick persons, will do mad tricks sometimes.

LADY EXAMINATION
And there are several sorts of Ayr, as there are several sorts of Drinks, some colder, some hotter, some moist, and some hath dry effects, and some Ayr refreshes and quenches heat, other some dissipates and expels cold, some revives the Spirits, and some inrages them, some corrupts Bodyes, and some preserves them.

MATRON
By my Faith, I perceive Ayr and Drink have many good and bad qualities, but I had rather have good Drink and bad Ayr, than bad Drink and good Ayr, there is some substance in the one, but the other is like unto that which I have heard of but could never see, which is Incorporality; for that which is not subject to my sight, I can hardly believe it is any thing.

LADY CENSURER
Indeed very thin Ayr is next unto nothing.

[Exeunt.

SCENE XIV

Enter **TWO GENTLEMEN**.

FIRST GENTLEMAN
Tom. Adventurer is gone to be a Souldier.

SECOND GENTLEMAN
Yes, and he may chance to get a glorious Fame.

FIRST GENTLEMAN
But particular Fames are like particular Creatures, some dye and decay sooner than others, but few live to old Nestors years, and some lye Bedrid, and a great Company are decrepid and lame, others are croked and deformed from their Birth, and some by evill Fortune; and many are Orphans, and aboundance Bastards and Changlings; and though War makes the lowdest noise in Fames Palace, yet Wit for the most part lives the longest therein; for Wit is such a delightfull Company, and such pleasant pastime, as old Father Time takes great care to preserve it, lapping Wit warm in the Memory, and feeding it often with Rehersals.

[Exeunt.

SCENE XV

Enter the **LADY EXAMINATION**, and the **LADY SOLITARY**.

LADY EXAMINATION
Come, Come, you will never get you a real Lover, if you delight so much in Solitaries.

LADY SOLITARY
I desire none: for real Lovers do oftentimes prove unconstant, whereas feigned lovers are as constant as the Contemplator would have them, and as many as they would have; besides, a crowd or multitude of thoughts may rise up in the brain; and be as Spectators of one single thought, which if the Contemplator pleases may be a Lover, and the rest of the Spectators thoughts may censure of that single thought, as of his good parts, or bad, his virtues, or vices, some may praise, others dispraise, and the like; thus a Contemplator can never want Lovers, Admirers, Censurers, nor any other Company, since the Mind can present them with what thoughts they desire, not only the thoughts of Men Women and Children, but of any other Creatures that Nature hath made; for why should not our Spirits or Soul delight and content us, without the real possession of outward Good, as well as the Spirits or Soul doth torment us with a real Evill? for why may not Opinion, or Fancy, as well and as much delight us, as Opinion and Fancy affright us, as they often do?

LADY EXAMINATION
But an over-studious Mind doth waste the Body, for the Thoughts feeds as much upon the Body, as the Body upon the meat we eat, and the Body nourishes the Thoughts as much as meat nourishes the Body, and for the most part, as the Body is effected so is the Mind, for a distempered Body makes a distempered Mind, as a Luxurious Body makes an Amorous Mind; and a Feavour in the Body makes the mind frantick, for the heat of a Feavour is like Strong-water, it makes the Spirits drunk, the Thoughts dizie, and the Mind sick.

LADY SOLITARY
Indeed the Body and the Mind do most commonly agree, as in Monarchy the King and the Subjects do, the Subjects obeying the King, and the King commanding the Subjects, yet sometimes the Subjects compel the King, and sometimes the King forces the Subjects, so sometimes the Appetite compels the Reason, at other times the Reason forces the Appetite to a Moderation, and sometimes the Humours of the Body which are like the senceless Commonalty, and the Passions of the Soul, which are as the Nobles, oftentimes fall out, where sometimes the Humours of the Body usurp with an uprore the Passions of the Soul, and sometimes the Passions overcome the Humours by a wise policy; but when as the Kingdome of Man is in Peace, the Imaginations in the head send down thoughts, as metal into the heart, wherein they are melted and minted into current Coin, each thought as each peece having a several stamp, some is stamped with Hate, some Spight, others Malice; some with Jealousy, some Hope, some with Fear, some Pitty, some Love, but that of Love is of the highest vallew; but these Coins serve for Commerce and Traffick in the Body, from the Authority of the Mind or Soul, whose stamp or Image each piece bears.

[Exeunt.

SCENE XVI

Enter **SIR WILLIAM ADMIRER**, and the **LADY PEACEABLE**.

SIR WILLIAM ADMIRER
Dear Mistriss how I love you!

LADY PEACEABLE
I wish I had Merits worthy your Affections.

SIR WILLIAM ADMIRER
You are all a man can wish in women kind, for you are young, fair, virtuous, witty and wise.

LADY PEACEABLE
Alas all youth hath more follies than years, whereas those that are old, have or ought to have more years than follies.

SIR WILLIAM ADMIRER
You might be thought old by your speech and actions, by reason you speak so experienced, and act with such prudence and discretion; wherefore I should judge you were instructed by those that are old, and knew much.

LADY PEACEABLE
Indeed my Educators were Aged, and my Tutors, like as Painters, drew with the Pencil of the Tongue, and the Colours of Sense, and the white of Truth, on the Platform of my Brain, many figurate discourses for the Understanding to view, but my Understanding hath weak Eyes.

SIR WILLIAM ADMIRER
Your Understanding neither wants sight nor light, but the Lady Faction wants both, or else she had not been so uncivil to you as she was when I was with you last; were not you very Cholerick with her?

LADY PEACEABLE
I am of too Melancholy a Nature to be very Cholerick.

SIR WILLIAM ADMIRER
Why, are those that are Melancholy never Cholerick?

LADY PEACEABLE
I cannot say never, but yet very seldome, by reason they want that heat which makes Choler; for though the Spirits of Melancholy persons may be as quick as those that are Cholerick, yet they are not so fiery, for there is as much difference betwixt Melancholy and Choler, as freesing and burning, the one contracts into a sad silence, the other expulses in blows, and many extravagant actions, and angry words; but those persons which are seldome angry, as all Melancholy persons are, who are of a patient, peaceable Nature, yet when they are angry are very angry; so those persons that are naturally Melancholy, that are seldome seen to be merry or to laugh, yet when they are merry, their mirth is ridiculous, and they will laugh extremely, as at nothing, or at any thing; so those that are naturally Contemplative, when they do speak, they speak beyond all sense and reason, their speech flows like as a Torrent, rough and forceable; thus we may perceive that extremes one way run into extremes another way.

SIR WILLIAM ADMIRER
I can truly witness that you are not apt to be angry, or at least not to appear angry; for I did wonder at your humble behaviour, civil answers, patient demeanors towards the Lady Faction.

LADY PEACEABLE

I may suffer an injury patiently when I cannot avoid it, but I will never injure my self in doing such actions, or speaking such words as are unbefitting, unworthy and base.

[Exeunt.

ACT V

SCENE XVII

Enter the **LADY SOLITARY**, her Governess a Grave **MATRON**, and a **GENTLEMAN** as coming a Journey.

MATRON
Pray Charge, thank this Gentleman for his gifts and favours to me.

LADY SOLITARY
Governess, let me tell you, that they do themselves a courtesy or favour that do a courtesy or favour to another; and therefore there needs no thanks.

GENTLEMAN
But Lady you ought to thank me, for coming out of my way so far as I have done to see you.

LADY SOLITARY
No truly, for if you came out of your way to see me, if it were for affection, it is a duty to Love, if for gratitude, it 'tis a duty to Obligation, if for civility, it 'tis a duty to Honour, if for Charity, it 'tis a duty to Heaven, and where a duty is due, the owner receives but his own when 'tis paid; wherefore it were a vain and extravagant civility, like unto madness, to give thanks for what is justly their own.

GENTLEMAN
I do confess Lady I am yours, and therefore whatsoever I do, the best of my actions is due to you, and I repent for saying you ought to thank me for comming out of my way to see you, and I crave your pardon for my error, and ask forgiveness for my fault.

LADY SOLITARY
I will forgive you, so I may be rid of you, for I love not Company but Solitariness.

[Exeunt.

SCENE XVIII

Enter the **LADY GADDER**, the **LADY KINDELING**, and the **LADY BRIDLEHEAD**.

LADY BRIDLEHEAD
Sir William Admirer is like Argus, stuck full of Eyes, but Sir William 's are the Eyes of fair Ladyes that gaze upon him.

LADY GADDER

The truth is, when he is in the Company of our Sex, all the women gaze on him.

LADY KINDELING

They may look if they please, and admire him, but I can assure them he loves and admires but one, which is the Lady Peaceable.

LADY GADDER

Why, is he in love with the Lady Peaceable?

LADY KINDELING

So much as he is to be married to her within two or three dayes.

LADY GADDER

I thought he had loved the Lady Faction.

LADY KINDLING

No, no, for he denies that ever he had any Matrimonial love for her.

LADY BRIDLEHEAD

Will they make a publick wedding?

LADY KINDELING

No, 'tis said the wedding will be kept private.

[Exeunt.

SCENE XIX

Enter the **LADY CENSURER**, the **LADY EXAMINATION**, and the **LADY SOLITARY**.

LADY EXAMINATION

Where have you been Lady Censurer?

LADY CENSURER

Faith at Court, amongst a Company of Ladyes and their Gallants.

LADY EXAMINATION

And what was their pastime?

LADY CENSURER

Why Singing, Dancing, Laughing, and Jesting; but I have earned an Angel amongst them.

LADY EXAMINATION

How prethee?

LADY CENSURER
Although not by the sweat of my brows, yet by the expence of my Spirits.

LADY EXAMINATION
Prethee tell.

LADY CENSURER
Why the Court Ladyes in a scornfull jesting, for Courtiers love to put persons out of Countenance if they can, prayed me to sing an old Song out of a new Ballad, as knowing my voice fit for no better Songs; but I told them, that if I did sing they should pay me for my pains; for there was never a blind Beggar, or poor young Wench, that sings at a door, but had somthing given them; they told me they would give me a penny, I answered, that when they sung to Gentlemen or Ladyes gates, that they had a shilling at least given them, and unless they would give me twelvepence apiece, I would not sing; so they out of a laughing sport, borrowed a Crown of the Gentlemen to give me.

LADY SOLITARY
Oh that's the Court fashion, for the women to borrow of the men.

LADY CENSURER
How should they live if they did not so? for in my Conscience they could not have made up twelve pence amongst a douzen of them, not in money; for their Clothes though costly and rich, yet are worn upon trust; but as I said, I was to sing them a Song for my money; so I sung them an old Song, the burden of the Song, Oh women, women, monstrous women, what do you mean for to do? but because the Song was against women, they would have had me given them their money back again, I told them no I would not, for it was lawfull gain for me to keep it, since I gained it by an honest industry, and that those that made a bargain must stick to it; then they told me, that if I would sing them a good old Song, they would give me another Crown; I told them I would have the money in hand, for fear they should dislike my Song when I had sung it, or at least to seem to dislike it, to save their money; so although they were loth, yet at last they borrowed another Crown to give me, thinking it did disgrace me, in that my voyce was fit for nothing but old Ballads, for all their Admirers, and Courtly Servants, or Servants for Courtship were with them; so then I sung them Doctor Faustus that gave his Soul away to the Devill; for I knew Conjurers and Devils pleased women best.

LADY EXAMINATION
They fright women.

LADY CENSURER
By your favour, all Conjurers gain more by womens coming to them to know their Fortunes, and for to find our losses, than they do by men; for where one man goeth to a Conjurer or Fortune-teller, their goeth a hundred women; but as I have told you, I sung the Song of Doctor Faustus.

LADY SOLITARY
For my part, I had rather hear a plain old Song, than any Italian, or French Love Songs stuff'd with Trilloes.

LADY CENSURER

That's strange, when as in those Harmonious Songs the wisest Poets, and skillfull'st Musicians, are joyned to make up one Song, and the most excellent voices are chosen to sing them.

LADY SOLITARY
I know not, but I am sooner weary to hear a famous and Artificial Singer sing than they are themselves with singing, for I hate their Quavers, demy, and semy Quavers, their Minnums, Crochets, and the like.

LADY EXAMINATION
The truth is, I have observed that when an old Ballad is plainly sung, most hearers will lissen with more delight, than to Italian and French Singers, although they sing with art and skill.

LADY SOLITARY
The most famous singer in these latter times I have heard in France, it was a woman, and an Italian sent for into France, where she was presented with very rich gifts for her rare singing, yet I durst a-laid my life for a wager, that there were more that could have taken more delight to hear an old Ballad sung, which Ballads are true stories put into verses and set to a Tune, than in all there Italian and French Love whining Songs, and languishing tunes.

LADY EXAMINATION
Well, but what will you do with your gettings?

LADY CENSURER
Faith I will go home and consider, and the next time I will tell you how I will imploy my ten shillings.

[Exeunt.

SCENE XX

Enter **TWO GENTLEMEN**.

FIRST GENTLEMAN
What makes you Booted and Spurred, are you going out of the town?

SECOND GENTLEMAN
Yes faith, I am going to a wedding, Swich and Spur.

FIRST GENTLEMAN
What, art thou going to be married?

SECOND GENTLEMAN
No, I am not so hasty, for though I can spur to another mans wedding, I cannot be spurred to my own.

FIRST GENTLEMAN
Whose wedding are you riding to?

SECOND GENTLEMAN

To Sir William Admirers, and the Lady Peaceable.

FIRST GENTLEMAN
Faith their names and marriage do disagree; for never did Husband after the first Month Admire his Wife, nor a Wife after two Months live Peaceably.

[Exeunt.

SCENE XXI

Enter the **LADY SOLITARY**, the **LADY EXAMINATION**, and the **LADY CENSURER**.

LADY EXAMINATION
How have you imployed the ten shillings got by singing?

LADY CENSURER
I must tell you, I have been extremely troubled how to imploy it, insomuch as my Mind hath never been at rest; for their hath been such arguing and disputing and contradiction amongst my Thoughts, as I did verily believe there would have been a mutiny in my head: for first I did resolve to put my ten shillings to pious uses, and then I thought to build some Alms Houses, as building one long room like a Gallery, making in it several Partitions, and the outward dores all a-like; these Houses, or rather partitioned rooms, for poor old and infirm persons, that could not work nor beg for their livelyhood, to live in; but when I had well considered, that when I had built my Alms Houses, which is as I said one long Room divided by Partitions, I should have nothing left to maintain them, and they to have only House-room, and have neither Meat, Drink, Clothes, nor Firing to feed them and to keep them from the injuries of the cold, having neither Fires nor Beds, I thought the Parish wherein they were Born, would better provide for them, so that instead of praying for me, they would Curse me; besides I considered, that after I was dead, had I means to leave an allowance, yet when it came for the Magistrates to chuse, those that should be put in they would leave out, and chuse idle young Huswives, or foul Sluts to dwell therein, such as those Magistrates would visit sometimes, to see what they did want, so as I let that design pass; then I thought to build a Church, and much were my thoughts concerned, whether the Roof should be flat, or vaulted, or sloping; but after I had resolved how the Roof should be, and where the Belfrey and Quest-room, I was sore perplex'd in my Mind, as where or how to place the Pulpit, whether at the East or West end, or at a Corner in the Church, or at one of the sides of the Church close by the Wall, but at last I resolved it should be placed in the midst of the Church, in the very Centre, that the voice of the Minister might spread round to the Circumference, so as all the Congregation might hear him; but when I considered that when my Church was built there was neither Benefices, Lands, nor Tithes, nor any allowance for the Minister, and that there was none that did or will preach meerly for Gods sake, but for gains sake, as to have a maintenance thereby, or some advancement therefrom, I desisted from that design; then I thought to build a Bedlam, and be the Keeper my self, but I considered that if any of the mad folkes should get loose, they might kill me, besides they stink so horribly, and require so much cleansing, not being capable of keeping themselves clean, as I resolved not to go forward with that design; then I thought to build a free School, and I to be the chief Tutoress my self, but when I remembred the confused noise the Scholars make reading all at once, that neither I could hear nor they understand what they read, I thought it would be to no purpose, because the Scholars would profit but little by their reading, and then I should be thought an ignorant Tutoress; at last I thought to give my ten

shillings to the poor Beggars, but when I considered the Alms that was given to Beggars did more harm than good, causing them to be idle and lazy, and incouraged them to go roving and Roguing about, I chang'd my Mind from that Act, but finding I could not imploy my ten shilligns in any pious Act, I thought to imploy it in something to be remembred by, as for Fame, whereupon I resolved to build a Pyramide or Cross, the Pyramide to be vastly high, and the Cross to be gloriously gilt, but then fearing a Rebellion, and knowing that in a Rebellion a Confused and superstitious rout, would certainly pull them down to the ground, and that when the Cross or Pyramide was down, I should be utterly forgotten, I desisted from that design; so finding as little imployment for my money to any famous act as to any pious use, I resolved to imploy it to my profit, so then I had a design to set up a Shop of small wares, but when I considered how dead Trading was, and how fast Tradesmen did break, and instead of being inriched became poorer than when first they begun, for to set up a Trade requires some stock, but when they break, they have not only lost their stock, but owe more than ever their stock was, so I went from that design; then I intended to buy me a parcell of Land with my ten shillings, but hearing there was much danger in buying of Land, for that many have morgaged their Lands to one, and sold them to another, or by an old Deed that hath layen in some old Trunck, Desk, or Box, which may be brought forth to claim the Land again, so as I must be forced to go to Law for my Land I bought, which would cost me more than my Lands, besides the infinite pains and trouble in following my Law Sute, and vext with querkes, and quillets Lawyers find to prolong the Sute, or else I must let my Land go, so lose it, finding this, I thought to put my money out to use, but then I considered that first I had only a piece of Parchment for my money, besides, it is a general rule that few or none take up money at use, but those that are Banckrouts, and when they had once got my money into their hands, I should neither get Use or Principal, for should I Imprison them, I should be never the neerer to get my money, for where there is nothing to be had, sayes the old Proverb, the King must lose his right; after this I intended to build a Ship, and Traffick with it on the Seas, but then considering the Various Winds, the Tempestuous Storms, the rough Seas, the lurking Sands, the dreadfull Rocks, the gaping Flouds that might split and swallow my Ship, and be drowned my self, I was resolved not to follow that design; then I thought to buy a place at Court, but when I considered how I must cringe and creep, flatter, rail, and be factious, and at last the expences at Court would be more than the profit of my place, by which I should become a Beggar, or at least a Shark, I left off that design; but after all these considerations I concluded with my self that the most profitablest way to imploy my ten shillings was to build a Bawdy-house, for I was sure that as soon as ever it was built Customers would resort thereunto; besides it was the most certain gain that was, without any expences, whereas all other Trades or Professions require means or stocks to begin with, whereas in these Professions or Trade the poorest may set up without borrowing or begging, for a stock to begin with; neither can alterations of times ruin it, for in all times whether Peace or Wars, and in all Nations, this Trade never fails, whereunto if you please to come Ladyes, you shall be very welcome.

LADY SOLITARY
It will not agree with my humour, for I love Solitariness, and there will be too much Company.

LADY CENSURER
There may be a great resort, but their Conversation is by single Couples.

LADY EXAMINATION
You are a wag Lady Censurer.

[Exeunt.

Enter **FOUR GENTLEMEN**.

FIRST GENTLEMAN
If I were to chuse a Wife, I would chuse the Lady Solitary.

SECOND GENTLEMAN
Why?

FIRST GENTLEMAN
Because those that are Solitary love not much Company, and being alone love not much noise, and loving no noise, love silence, and loving silence, love not to talk, so as in having of her, I shall have a Solitary, Peaceable, Quiet, Silent Wife.

THIRD GENTLEMAN
And if I were to chuse, I would chuse the Lady Censurer, for she would let nothing pass her judgment: for she will give her opinion of all things, persons, and actions; so in having her to my Wife, I should have a general Intelligencer, or at least her opinion of all things.

SECOND GENTLEMAN
But if her Judgment were not good, her opinion would be erroneous.

THIRD GENTLEMAN
I care not, it would serve to pass an idle time with.

FOURTH GENTLEMAN
And if I might chuse, I would chuse the Lady Examination for a Wife.

SECOND GENTLEMAN
Why?

FOURTH GENTLEMAN
Because she knows most humours and passages of every body, and their affairs, so by her I should be entertained with news from all places, as of all actions done, opinions held, words spoke, or thoughts thought.

SECOND GENTLEMAN
I would I could have my wish as easily, as you might have your choice.

FIRST GENTLEMAN
What would you wish?

SECOND GENTLEMAN
I would wish to be unmarried, for if I were, I would never be troubled with a Wife again; but let me advise you, for I love to have married Companions, that you three should go a woing to those three Ladyes, they cannot nor will not deny your Sute, being all three of you rich, young and handsome.

ALL THREE
We will take your Counsel.

[Exeunt.

MARGARET CAVENDISH – A CONCISE BIBLIOGRAPHY

Philosophical Fancies (1653)
Poems and Fancies (1653)
Philosophical and Physical Opinions (1655)
Nature's Pictures drawn by Fancie's Pencil to the Life (1656)
The World's Olio (1655)
Playes, (1662) folio, containing twenty-one plays including
Loves Adventures
The Several Wits
Youths Glory, and Deaths Banquet
The Lady Contemplation
Wits Cabal
The Unnatural Tragedy
The Public Wooing
The Matrimonial Trouble
Nature's Three Daughters (Beauty, Love and Wit) Part I & Part II
The Religious
The Comical Hash
Bell in Campo
A Comedy of the Apocryphal Ladies
The Female Academy
Plays never before printed (1668), containing five plays.
The Sociable Companions, or the Female Wits
The Presence
The Bridals
The Convent of Pleasure
A Piece of a Play
Orations of Divers Sorts (1662)
Philosophical Letters, or Modest Reflections upon some Opinions in Natural Philosophy maintained by several learned authors of the age (1664)
CCXI Sociable Letters (1664)
Observations upon Experimental Philosophy & Description of a New World (1666)
The Blazing World (1666)
The Life of William Cavendish, Duke, Marquis, and Earl of Newcastle, Earl of Ogle, Viscount Mansfield, and Baron of Bolsover, of Ogle, Bothal, and Hepple, &c. (1667)
Grounds of Natural Philosophy (1668)